P9-DGW-813

BY ALLAN MOREY

THE DETROIT

LIONS

STORY

BELLWETHER MEDIA · MINNEAPOLIS, MN

TM

Are you ready to take it to the extreme? Torque books thrust you into the action-packed world of sports, vehicles, mystery, and adventure. These books may include dirt, smoke, fire, and chilling tales. **WARNING**: read at your own risk.

This edition first published in 2017 by Bellwether Media, Inc.

No part of this publication may be reproduced in whole or in part without written permission of the publisher. For information regarding permission, write to Bellwether Media, Inc., Attention: Permissions Department, 5357 Penn Avenue South, Minneapolis, MN 55419.

Library of Congress Cataloging-in-Publication Data

Names: Morey, Allan.
Title: The Detroit Lions Story / by Allan Morey.
Description: Minneapolis, MN : Bellwether Media, Inc., 2017. | Series:
   Torque: NFL Teams | Includes bibliographical references and index.
Identifiers: LCCN 2015036452 | ISBN 9781626173651 (hardcover : alk. paper)
Subjects: LCSH: Detroit Lions (Football team)–History–Juvenile literature.
Classification: LCC GV956.D4 M67 2017 | DDC 796.332/640977434–dc23
LC record available at http://lccn.loc.gov/2015036452

Printed in the United States of America, North Mankato, MN.

TABLE OF CONTENTS

It is Thanksgiving Day, 2013. The Detroit Lions face the Green Bay Packers. The game starts off slow. Near halftime, the score is tied 10 to 10.

BIG STATS
Matthew Stafford threw for more than 300 yards in the 2013 Thanksgiving Day game.

Reggie Bush

Then **running back** Reggie Bush bursts into the end zone at the last minute. Touchdown! The Lions take the lead against their **rival**.

Early in the third quarter, **quarterback** Matthew Stafford passes the ball to **wide receiver** Calvin Johnson. Johnson runs into the end zone to score!

The Lions' **defense** shuts down the Packers' **offense**. They do not give up another point. But the Lions keep on scoring. By the end of the game, it is 40 to 10. Lions win!

Calvin Johnson

SCORING TERMS

END ZONE

the area at each end of a football field; a team scores by entering the opponent's end zone with the football.

EXTRA POINT

a score that occurs when a kicker kicks the ball between the opponent's goal posts after a touchdown is scored; 1 point.

FIELD GOAL

a score that occurs when a kicker kicks the ball between the opponent's goal posts; 3 points.

SAFETY

a score that occurs when a player on offense is tackled behind his own goal line; 2 points for defense.

TOUCHDOWN

a score that occurs when a team crosses into its opponent's end zone with the football; 6 points.

TWO-POINT CONVERSION

a score that occurs when a team crosses into its opponent's end zone with the football after scoring a touchdown; 2 points.

The Lions are known for their Silver Stretch offense of the 1990s. The team had speedy receivers and a great running back. These players spread out defenses on the field.

Barry Sanders rushing, 1994

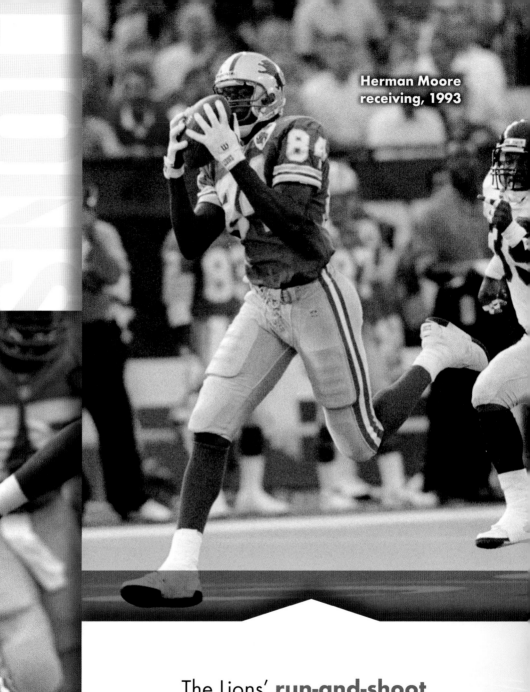

Herman Moore receiving, 1993

The Lions' **run-and-shoot** style of play was fast-paced. Defenses struggled to stop them from scoring.

SUPER BOWL HOST

In 2006, Ford Field hosted Super Bowl 40. In that game, the Pittsburgh Steelers beat the Seattle Seahawks 21 to 10.

Detroit, Michigan, is called the "Motor City." This is because Henry Ford set up an auto factory there. It is where the Model T car was first built.

The Lions have strong ties to the Ford family. In 1963, Henry Ford's grandson became the team's main owner. The Lions' stadium is also named Ford Field.

DETROIT,
MICHIGAN

N
W—E
S

FORD FIELD

HOME OF THE DETROIT LIONS

DEFEND
THE DEN

Call 313-262-2222 for details

11

The Lions joined the National Football League (NFL) in 1930 as the Portsmouth Spartans. Today, they play in the National Football **Conference** (NFC). They are in the North **Division**.

This division has some of the NFL's oldest teams. It includes the Green Bay Packers and Chicago Bears. The Minnesota Vikings also play in the North.

NFL DIVISIONS

AFC

AFC NORTH

BALTIMORE **RAVENS**

CINCINNATI **BENGALS**

CLEVELAND **BROWNS**

PITTSBURGH **STEELERS**

AFC EAST

BUFFALO **BILLS**

MIAMI **DOLPHINS**

NEW ENGLAND **PATRIOTS**

NEW YORK **JETS**

AFC SOUTH

HOUSTON **TEXANS**

INDIANAPOLIS **COLTS**

JACKSONVILLE **JAGUARS**

TENNESSEE **TITANS**

AFC WEST

DENVER **BRONCOS**

KANSAS CITY **CHIEFS**

OAKLAND **RAIDERS**

SAN DIEGO **CHARGERS**

 **NFC**

NFC NORTH

 CHICAGO
BEARS

 DETROIT
LIONS

 GREEN BAY
PACKERS

 MINNESOTA
VIKINGS

NFC EAST

DALLAS
COWBOYS

 GIANTS

 PHILADELPHIA
EAGLES

 WASHINGTON
REDSKINS

NFC SOUTH

 FALCONS

 CAROLINA
PANTHERS

NEW ORLEANS
SAINTS

 BUCCANEERS

NFC WEST

 CARDINALS

 LOS ANGELES
RAMS

 SAN FRANCISCO
49ERS

 SEATTLE
SEAHAWKS

In 1934, radio executive George Richards bought the Portsmouth Spartans. He moved the football team to Detroit. He renamed it the Lions. The next year, the Lions became NFL champions!

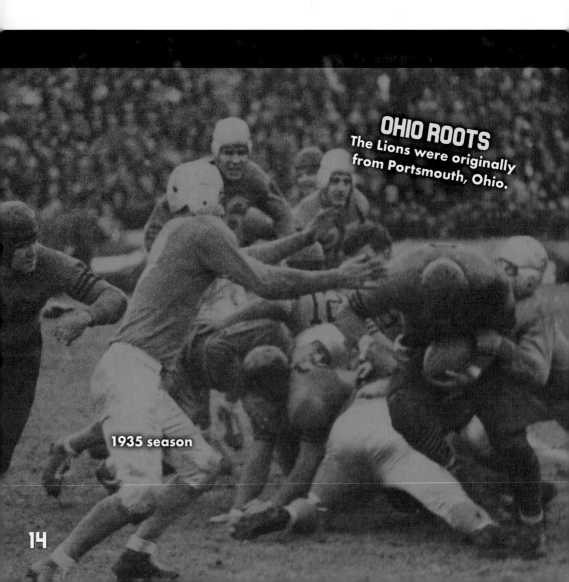

OHIO ROOTS
The Lions were originally from Portsmouth, Ohio.

1935 season

The 1950s were successful years for the Lions. A tough defense helped them claim three more NFL Championships.

WORST SEASON EVER
In 2008, the Lions became the only team to lose all 16 games in a season.

The Lions have struggled in recent years. After their NFL Championship in 1957, they did not win a **playoff** game again until after the 1991 season.

Today, Lions fans have high hopes. The team reached the playoffs after 2011 and 2014.

2014
season

ROSS
12

LIONS TIMELINE

1930
Joined the NFL (as the Portsmouth Spartans)

1934
Moved to Detroit, Michigan, and changed name to the Lions

1953
Won second straight NFL Championship, beating the Cleveland Browns

17 FINAL SCORE **16**

1934
Played in their first Thanksgiving Day game

1935
Won their first NFL Championship, beating the New York Giants

26 FINAL SCORE **7**

1957
Won the NFL Championship, beating the Cleveland Browns

59 FINAL SCORE **14**

1989

Drafted Hall-of-Fame
running back Barry Sanders

2007

Drafted wide receiver
Calvin Johnson

2002

First played at Ford Field

2009

Drafted quarterback
Matthew Stafford

LIONS

Dutch Clark was the Lions' first star player. He was a running back. But he also played quarterback and **kicker**. He helped the Lions win their first championship.

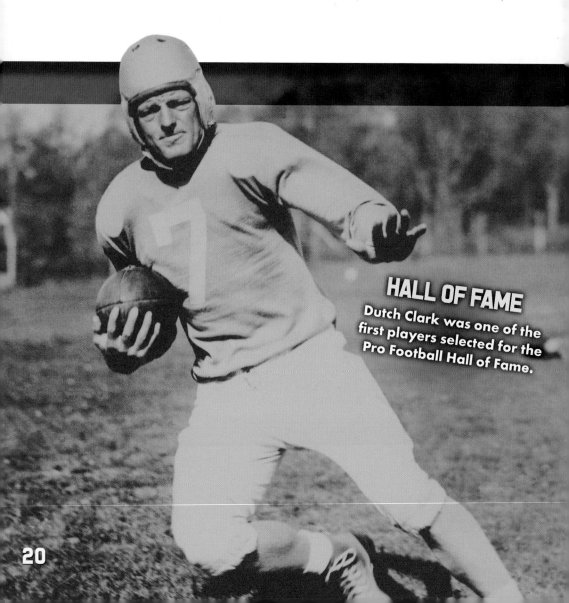

HALL OF FAME
Dutch Clark was one of the first players selected for the Pro Football Hall of Fame.

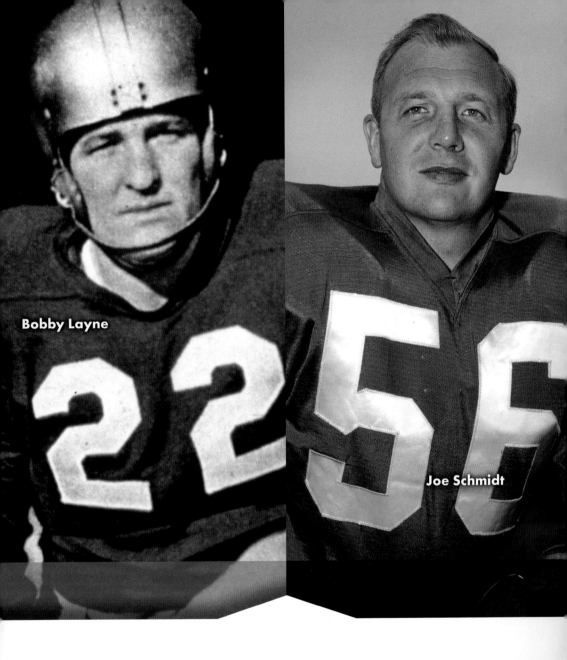

Bobby Layne

Joe Schmidt

In the 1950s, the Lions had many great players. Quarterback Bobby Layne led the offense. **Linebacker** Joe Schmidt was a force on defense.

In 1989, the Lions **drafted** one of the all-time best running backs. Barry Sanders **rushed** for more than 15,000 yards with the team! Recently, Matthew Stafford and Calvin Johnson were a great quarterback-wide receiver combination. Stafford threw more than 50 touchdown passes to Johnson. Golden Tate is the new wide receiver target.

TEAM GREATS

EARL "DUTCH" CLARK
RUNNING BACK,
QUARTERBACK, KICKER
1931-1932, 1934-1938

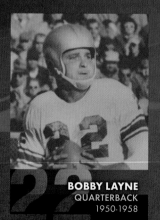

BOBBY LAYNE
QUARTERBACK
1950-1958

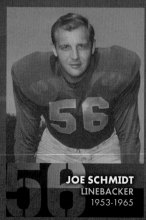

JOE SCHMIDT
LINEBACKER
1953-1965

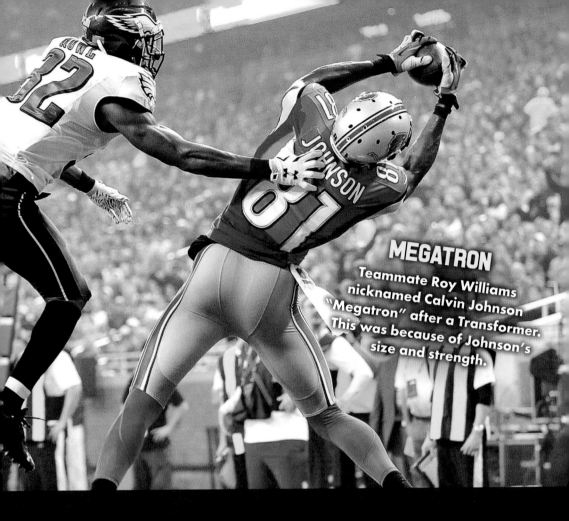

MEGATRON

Teammate Roy Williams nicknamed Calvin Johnson "Megatron" after a Transformer. This was because of Johnson's size and strength.

BARRY SANDERS
RUNNING BACK
1989-1998

CALVIN JOHNSON
WIDE RECEIVER
2007-2015

MATTHEW STAFFORD
QUARTERBACK
2009-PRESENT

Back in the 1930s, more people watched baseball than football. George Richards wanted to change that. In 1934, he set up a special football game on Thanksgiving Day.

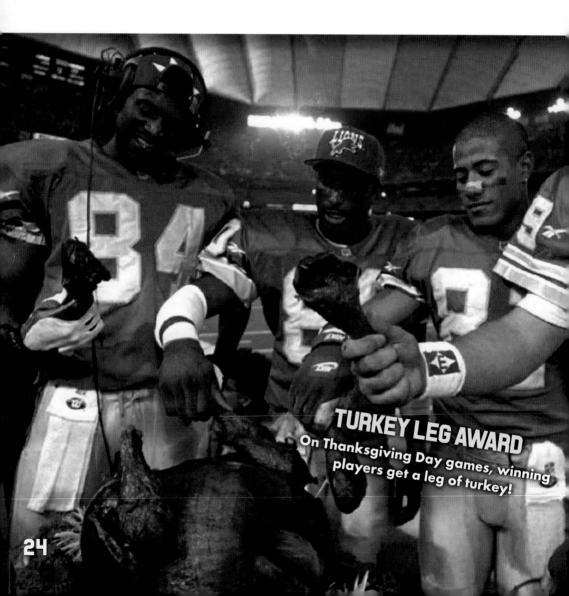

TURKEY LEG AWARD
On Thanksgiving Day games, winning players get a leg of turkey!

The Lions lost to the Bears that day. But it was a start of a popular tradition. The Lions always look forward to playing on Thanksgiving Day.

The Lions have had little success recently. But that does not stop people from cheering them on. Their fans are proud of the team's long history.

And every year, the Lions will continue to serve up their special holiday treat. Millions of football fans from all over will tune in to watch them play on Turkey Day.

MORE ABOUT THE
LIONS

Team name:
Detroit Lions

Team name explained:
**Named to go with
Detroit's baseball team,
the Tigers**

Nicknames:
**The Silver Rush,
Silver Stretch**

Joined NFL: 1930

Conference: NFC

Division: North

**Main rivals: Green Bay
Packers, Minnesota Vikings**

Hometown:
Detroit, Michigan

Training camp location: Headquarters & Training Facility, Allen Park, Michigan

DETROIT

MICHIGAN

N W E S

Home stadium name: **Ford Field**

Stadium opened: **2002**

Seats in stadium: **65,000**

Logo: **A blue lion**

Colors: **Blue, silver, black, white**

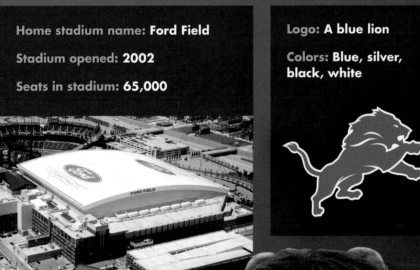

Mascot: **Roary**

GLOSSARY

conference—a large grouping of sports teams that often play one another

defense—the group of players who try to stop the opposing team from scoring

division—a small grouping of sports teams that often play one another; usually there are several divisions of teams in a conference.

TO LEARN MORE

AT THE LIBRARY

Bodden, Valerie. *Calvin Johnson*. Mankato, Minn.: Creative Education, Creative Paperbacks, 2015.

Burgess, Zack. *Meet the Detroit Lions*. Chicago, Ill.: Norwood House Press, 2016.

Teitelbaum, Michael. *NFC North*. Mankato, Minn.: Child's World, 2012.

ON THE WEB

Learning more about the Detroit Lions is as easy as 1, 2, 3.

1. Go to www.factsurfer.com.

2. Enter "Detroit Lions" into the search box.

3. Click the "Surf" button and you will see a list of related web sites.

With factsurfer.com, finding more information is just a click away.

INDEX